I HAVE DIABETES, AND IT'S OKAY!

Written by

Dr. William M. Bauer

Illustrated by

Mallory Hill

WestBow Press books may be ordered through booksellers or by contacting:

WestBow Press
A Division of Thomas Nelson & Zondervan
1663 Liberty Drive
Bloomington, IN 47403
www.westbowpress.com
844-714-3454

Interior Image Credit: Mallory Hill

ISBN: 978-1-6642-3770-4 (sc)
ISBN: 978-1-6642-3771-1 (e)

Library of Congress Control Number: 2021912493

Print information available on the last page.

WestBow Press rev. date: 07/21/2021

WESTBOW
PRESS®
A DIVISION OF THOMAS NELSON
& ZONDERVAN

I HAVE DIABETES, AND IT'S OKAY!

About the Author:

Dr. William M. (Bill) Bauer is a licensed clinical counselor in the rural Mid-Ohio Valley area who was a former classroom teacher, principal, and college professor. He has worked children and adults with disabilities all of his life and hopes that this book brings an understanding of children with disabilities, their teachers, and their classmates.

THIS BOOK IS DEDICATED TO:

ALL PEOPLE WITH DISABILITIES WHOSE LIVES ARE SHARED IN THIS BOOK SERIES TO MAKE THE WORLD A BETTER PLACE. ALL WE WANT IS TO BE ACCEPTED AS WE ARE, HAVE FRIENDS, LIVE IN OUR COMMUNITIES AND TO DREAM AS OUR NON-DISABLED PEERS.

SPECIAL THANKS TO MY WIFE, MARY ELLA, DAUGHTER MADISON RYSER, HER HUSBAND ANDREW AND GRANDSON JACK.

#GRANTSPEED.
LOVE YOU, SON

Forewords:

I have had the pleasure of working with Dr. Bauer in the professional education and mental health fields for over two decades, and this book series is his latest outstanding work to help young people understand and accept differences. Each title focuses on a uniqueness and assures us that "it is OKAY!"

Dr. Stephanie Starcher
Public School Superintendent

Being different is OK! Every effort to erase stigma surrounding our differences is important. The earlier we start, the better chance we have at preventing stigma from even occurring. I had the honor of meeting Dr. Bill Bauer when I was in college, and it is no surprise his work as a mental health advocate would transpire into this series of books. I'm thankful for his commitment to celebrating our differences.

Nick Gehlfuss, MFA, Actor, film and television.
Currently, Dr. Halstead, Chicago Med.

This book series by Dr. William Bauer — my good friend Bill — fills a niche in children's literature that embraces diversity and self esteem. This series is not only important, but extremely fun. As founder of Orphans International, I look forward to reading these stories to children of all faiths and abilities around the world. This book is indeed a living testament to Bill's own son. The world is a better place because of Bill Bauer! #GrantSpeed

James Jay Dudley Luce, Founder Orphans International Worldwide,
International Entrepreneur

MY NAME IS AUSTIN. I HAVE DIABETES, AND IT'S OKAY.

DIABETES MEANS THAT MY BODY DOESN'T MAKE ENOUGH INSULIN. INSULIN IS SOMETHING ALL PEOPLE HAVE TO HAVE TO LIVE.

WHEN I FIRST GOT DIABETES, I WAS ALWAYS HUNGRY, TIRED, HAD TO GO TO THE RESTROOM ALL OF THE TIME AND WAS LOSING WEIGHT WHEN I DIDN'T WANT TO.

MY MOM TOOK ME TO THE DOCTOR, AND THE DOCTOR DID A BUNCH OF TESTS. THE TESTS SHOWED THAT I HAVE JUVENILE DIABETES.

I NOW HAVE TO WATCH HOW MUCH SUGAR I EAT AND HOW MUCH EXERCISE I GET OR IT COULD HURT ME.

TO MAKE SURE I HAVE THE RIGHT AMOUNT OF INSULIN IN MY BODY, I HAVE TO TAKE SHOTS OF INSULIN OR I CAN USE A PUMP THAT WILL PUMP IT INTO MY STOMACH.

I CHECK MY SUGAR LEVELS FOUR TIMES A DAY. SOME PEOPLE CHECK THEIR LEVELS MORE SOME CHECK THEIR LEVELS LESS. I CHECK MINE WHEN I WAKE UP, AT NOON, AT DINNER AND BEFORE I GO TO BED.

MY PARENTS WENT TO MY SCHOOL TO TALK TO THE SCHOOL NURSE AND MY TEACHERS TO TELL THEM ABOUT DIABETES. WE DID A LITTLE SPEECH TO MY CLASS ABOUT DIABETES SO THAT ALL COULD UNDERSTAND.

When I feel tired or hungry, I test my sugar during the day by poking my finger with a small needle and testing my blood. It doesn't hurt.

DIABETES DOESN'T MAKE ME DIFFERENT THAN ANYONE ELSE. I JUST HAVE TO MAKE SURE I KEEP AN EYE ON IT.

I WANT TO BE A POLICE OFFICER WHEN I GROW UP AND DIABETES WILL NOT GET IN THE WAY.

MY NAME IS AUSTIN. I HAVE DIABETES, AND IT'S OKAY.

Printed in the United States
by Baker & Taylor Publisher Services